LOWER SUWANNEE NATIONAL WILDLIFE REFUGE

Comprehensive Conservation Plans

The following document articulates the broad strategy the President set forth in 2003 and provides an update on our progress as well as the challenges remaining.

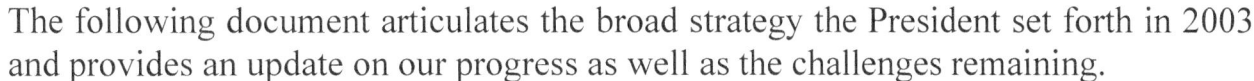

"The United States has no intention of determining the precise form of Iraq's new government. That choice belongs to the Iraqi people. Yet, we will ensure that one brutal dictator is not replaced by another. All Iraqis must have a voice in the new government, and all citizens must have their rights protected.

Rebuilding Iraq will require a sustained commitment from many nations, including our own: we will remain in Iraq as long as necessary, and not a day more."

- President George W. Bush, February 26, 2003

Table of Contents

OUR NATIONAL STRATEGY FOR VICTORY IN IRAQ:
Helping the Iraqi People Defeat the Terrorists and Build an Inclusive Democratic State

➤ <u>Victory in Iraq is Defined in Stages</u>
- **Short term**, Iraq is making steady progress in fighting terrorists, meeting political milestones, building democratic institutions, and standing up security forces.
- **Medium term**, Iraq is in the lead defeating terrorists and providing its own security, with a fully constitutional government in place, and on its way to achieving its economic potential.
- **Longer term**, Iraq is peaceful, united, stable, and secure, well integrated into the international community, and a full partner in the global war on terrorism.

➤ <u>Victory in Iraq is a Vital U.S. Interest</u>
- Iraq is the central front in the global war on terror. Failure in Iraq will embolden terrorists and expand their reach; success in Iraq will deal them a decisive and crippling blow.
- The fate of the greater Middle East – which will have a profound and lasting impact on American security – hangs in the balance.

➤ <u>Failure is Not an Option</u>
- Iraq would become a safe haven from which terrorists could plan attacks against America, American interests abroad, and our allies.
- Middle East reformers would never again fully trust American assurances of support for democracy and human rights in the region – a historic opportunity lost.
- The resultant tribal and sectarian chaos would have major consequences for American security and interests in the region.

➤ <u>The Enemy Is Diffuse and Sophisticated</u>
- The enemy is a combination of rejectionists, Saddamists, and terrorists affiliated with or inspired by Al Qaida. Distinct but integrated strategies are required to defeat each element.
- Each element shares a common short-term objective – to intimidate, terrorize, and tear down – but has separate and incompatible long-term goals.
- Exploiting these differences within the enemy is a key element of our strategy.

➤ <u>Our Strategy for Victory is Clear</u>
- We will help the Iraqi people build a new Iraq with a constitutional, representative government that respects civil rights and has security forces sufficient to maintain domestic order and keep Iraq from becoming a safe haven for terrorists. *To achieve this end, we are pursuing an integrated strategy along three broad tracks*, which together incorporate the efforts of the Iraqi government, the Coalition, cooperative countries in the region, the international community, and the United Nations.

- ***The Political Track*** involves working to forge a broadly supported national compact for democratic governance by helping the Iraqi government:
  - ✓ ***Isolate*** enemy elements from those who can be won over to the political process by countering false propaganda and demonstrating to all Iraqis that they have a stake in a democratic Iraq;
  - ✓ ***Engage*** those outside the political process and invite in those willing to turn away from violence through ever-expanding avenues of participation; and
  - ✓ ***Build*** stable, pluralistic, and effective national institutions that can protect the interests of all Iraqis, and facilitate Iraq's full integration into the international community.

- ***The Security Track*** involves carrying out a campaign to defeat the terrorists and neutralize the insurgency, developing Iraqi security forces, and helping the Iraqi government:
  - ✓ ***Clear*** areas of enemy control by remaining on the offensive, killing and capturing enemy fighters and denying them safe-haven;
  - ✓ ***Hold*** areas freed from enemy influence by ensuring that they remain under the control of the Iraqi government with an adequate Iraqi security force presence; and
  - ✓ ***Build*** Iraqi Security Forces and the capacity of local institutions to deliver services, advance the rule of law, and nurture civil society.

- ***The Economic Track*** involves setting the foundation for a sound and self-sustaining economy by helping the Iraqi government:
  - ✓ ***Restore*** Iraq's infrastructure to meet increasing demand and the needs of a growing economy;
  - ✓ ***Reform*** Iraq's economy, which in the past has been shaped by war, dictatorship, and sanctions, so that it can be self-sustaining in the future; and
  - ✓ ***Build*** the capacity of Iraqi institutions to maintain infrastructure, rejoin the international economic community, and improve the general welfare of all Iraqis.

➢ This Strategy is Integrated and its Elements are Mutually Reinforcing
  - Progress in each of the political, security, and economic tracks reinforces progress in the other tracks.
    - ✓ For instance, as the ***political process*** has moved forward, terrorists have become more isolated, leading to more intelligence on security threats from Iraqi citizens, which has led to ***better security*** in previously violent areas, a more stable infrastructure, the prospect of ***economic progress***, and expanding ***political participation***.

➢ Victory Will Take Time
  - **Our strategy is working:** Much has been accomplished in Iraq, including the removal of Saddam's tyranny, negotiation of an interim constitution, restoration of full sovereignty, holding of free national elections, formation of an elected government, drafting of a permanent constitution, ratification of that constitution, introduction of a sound currency, gradual restoration of neglected infrastructure, the ongoing training and equipping of Iraqi security forces, and the increasing capability of those forces to take on the terrorists and secure their nation.
  - **Yet many challenges remain:** Iraq is overcoming decades of a vicious tyranny, where governmental authority stemmed solely from fear, terror, and brutality.
    - ✓ It is not realistic to expect a fully functioning democracy, able to defeat its enemies and peacefully reconcile generational grievances, to be in place less than three years after Saddam was finally removed from power.
  - Our comprehensive strategy will help Iraqis overcome remaining challenges, but defeating the multi-headed enemy in Iraq – and ensuring that it cannot threaten Iraq's democratic gains once we leave – requires persistent effort across many fronts.

➢ Our Victory Strategy Is (and Must Be) Conditions Based
  - With resolve, victory will be achieved, although not by a date certain.
    - ✓ No war has ever been won on a timetable and neither will this one.
  - But lack of a timetable does not mean our posture in Iraq (both military and civilian) will remain static over time. As conditions change, our posture will change.
    - ✓ We expect, but cannot guarantee, that our force posture will change over the next year, as the political process advances and Iraqi security forces grow and gain experience.
    - ✓ While our military presence may become less visible, it will remain lethal and decisive, able to confront the enemy wherever it may organize.
    - ✓ Our mission in Iraq is to win the war. Our troops will return home when that mission is complete.

OUR NATIONAL STRATEGY FOR VICTORY IN IRAQ:
Helping the Iraqi People Defeat the Terrorists and Build an Inclusive Democratic State

PART I – STRATEGIC OVERVIEW

"Our mission in Iraq is clear. We're hunting down the terrorists. We're helping Iraqis build a free nation that is an ally in the war on terror. We're advancing freedom in the broader Middle East. We are removing a source of violence and instability, and laying the foundation of peace for our children and grandchildren."

-President George W. Bush, June 28, 2003

VICTORY IN IRAQ DEFINED

As the central front in the global war on terror, success in Iraq is an essential element in the long war against the ideology that breeds international terrorism. Unlike past wars, however, victory in Iraq will not come in the form of an enemy's surrender, or be signaled by a single particular event – there will be no Battleship Missouri, no Appomattox. The ultimate victory will be achieved in stages, and we expect:

➢ *In the short term*:

- An Iraq that is making steady progress in fighting terrorists and neutralizing the insurgency, meeting political milestones; building democratic institutions; standing up robust security forces to gather intelligence, destroy terrorist networks, and maintain security; and tackling key economic reforms to lay the foundation for a sound economy.

➢ *In the medium term*:

- An Iraq that is in the lead defeating terrorists and insurgents and providing its own security, with a constitutional, elected government in place, providing an inspiring example to reformers in the region, and well on its way to achieving its economic potential.

➢ *In the longer term*:

- An Iraq that has defeated the terrorists and neutralized the insurgency.

- An Iraq that is peaceful, united, stable, democratic, and secure, where Iraqis have the institutions and resources they need to govern themselves justly and provide security for their country.

- An Iraq that is a partner in the global war on terror and the fight against the proliferation of weapons of mass destruction, integrated into the international community, an engine for regional economic growth, and proving the fruits of democratic governance to the region.

VICTORY IN IRAQ IS A VITAL U.S. INTEREST

➤ The war on terrorism is the defining challenge of our generation, just as the struggle against communism and fascism were challenges of the generations before. As with those earlier struggles, the United States is fully committed to meeting this challenge. We will do everything it takes to win.

➤ **Prevailing in Iraq will help us win the war on terror.**

- *The terrorists regard Iraq as the central front in their war against humanity. And we must recognize Iraq as the central front in our war on terror.*

    - Osama Bin Laden has declared that the "third world war…is raging" in Iraq, and it will end there, in "either victory and glory, or misery and humiliation."

    - Bin Laden's deputy Ayman al-Zawahiri has declared Iraq to be "the place for the greatest battle," where he hopes to "expel the Americans" and then spread "the jihad wave to the secular countries neighboring Iraq."

    - Al Qaida in Iraq, led by Abu Musab al-Zarqawi, has openly declared that "we fight today in Iraq, and tomorrow in the Land of the Two Holy Places, and after there the west."

        ✓ *As the terrorists themselves recognize, the outcome in Iraq – success or failure – is critical to the outcome in the broader war on terrorism.*

- *What happens in Iraq will influence the fate of the Middle East for generations to come, with a profound impact on our own national security.*

    - Ceding ground to terrorists in one of the world's most strategic regions will threaten the world's economy and America's security, growth, and prosperity, for decades to come.

    - An emerging democracy in Iraq will change the regional status quo that for decades has bred alienation and spawned the transnational terrorism that targets us today.

    - The terrorists' perverse ideology is countered by the advance of freedom and the recognition that all people have the right to live under democracy and the rule of law, free from oppression and fear, with hope and optimism for the future.

THE BENEFITS OF VICTORY IN IRAQ

➤ Helping the people of Iraq is the morally right thing to do – America does not abandon its friends in the face of adversity. *Helping the people of Iraq, however, **is also in our own national interest**.*

➤ If we and our Iraqi partners prevail in Iraq, we will have made America:

- *Safer…*
  - by removing Saddam Hussein, a destabilizing force in a vital region, a ruthless dictator who had a history of pursuing and even using weapons of mass destruction, was a state sponsor of terror, had invaded his neighbors, and who was violently opposed to America;
  - by depriving terrorists of a safe haven from which they could plan and launch attacks against the United States and American interests;
  - by delivering a strategic setback to the terrorists and keeping them on the run;
  - by delivering a decisive blow to the ideology that fuels international terrorism, proving that the power of freedom is stronger than a perverse vision of violence, hatred, and oppression.

- *Stronger…*
  - by demonstrating to our friends and enemies the reliability of U.S. power, the strength of our commitment to our friends, and the tenacity of our resolve against our enemies;
  - by securing a new friend and partner in the fight against terrorism in the heart of the Middle East.

- *More Certain of its Future …*
  - politically, by bolstering democratic reformers – and the prospects for peaceful, democratic governments – in a region that for decades has been a source of instability and stagnation;
  - economically, by facilitating progressive reform in the region and depriving terrorists control over a hub of the world's economy.

THE CONSEQUENCES OF FAILURE

➢ If we and our Iraqi partners fail in Iraq, *Iraq will become*:

- A safe haven for terrorists as Afghanistan once was, only this time in some of the world's most strategic territory, with vast natural resources to exploit and to use to fund future attacks.

- A country where oppression – and the brutal imposition of inhumane practices, such as those of the Taliban in Afghanistan – is pervasive.

- A failed state and source of instability for the entire Middle East, with all the attendant risks and incalculable costs for American security and prosperity.

➢ Furthermore, if we and our Iraqi partners fail in Iraq, *the terrorists will have*:

- Won a decisive victory over the United States, vindicating their tactics of beheadings, suicide bombings, and ruthless intimidation of civilians, inviting more deadly attacks against Americans and other free people across the globe.

- Placed the American people in greater danger by destabilizing a vital region, weakening our friends, and clearing the way for terrorist attacks here at home. *The terrorists will be emboldened in their belief that America cannot stand and fight, but will cut and run in the face of adversity.*

- Called into question American credibility and commitment in the region and the world. Our friends and foes alike would doubt our staying power, and this would damage our efforts to counter other security threats and to advance other economic and political interests worldwide.

  ✓ *Since 1998, Al Qaida has repeatedly cited Vietnam, Beirut, and Somalia, as examples to encourage more attacks against America and our interests overseas.*

- Weakened the growing democratic impulses in the region. Middle East reformers would never again fully trust American assurances of support for democracy and pluralism in the region – *a historic opportunity, central to America's long-term security, forever lost.*

If we retreat from Iraq, the terrorists will pursue us and our allies, expanding the fight to the rest of the region and to our own shores.

OUR ENEMIES AND THEIR GOALS

➢ The enemy in Iraq is a combination of rejectionists, Saddamists, and terrorists affiliated with or inspired by Al Qaida. These three groups share a common opposition to the elected Iraqi government and to the presence of Coalition forces, but otherwise have separate and to some extent incompatible goals.

- **Rejectionists** are the largest group. They are largely Sunni Arabs who have not embraced the shift from Saddam Hussein's Iraq to a democratically governed state. Not all Sunni Arabs fall into this category. But those that do are against a new Iraq in which they are no longer the privileged elite. Most of these rejectionists opposed the new constitution, but many in their ranks are recognizing that opting out of the democratic process has hurt their interests.

  ✓ *We judge that over time many in this group will increasingly support a democratic Iraq provided that the federal government protects minority rights and the legitimate interests of all communities.*

- **Saddamists and former regime loyalists** harbor dreams of reestablishing a Ba'athist dictatorship and have played a lead role in fomenting wider sentiment against the Iraqi government and the Coalition.

  ✓ *We judge that few from this group can be won over to support a democratic Iraq, but that this group can be marginalized to the point where it can and will be defeated by Iraqi forces.*

- **Terrorists affiliated with or inspired by Al Qaida** make up the smallest enemy group but are the most lethal and pose the most immediate threat because **(1)** they are responsible for the most dramatic atrocities, which kill the most people and function as a recruiting tool for further terrorism and **(2)** they espouse the extreme goals of Osama Bin Laden – chaos in Iraq which will allow them to establish a base for toppling Iraq's neighbors and launching attacks outside the region and against the U.S. homeland.

✓ *The terrorists have identified Iraq as central to their global aspirations. For that reason, terrorists and extremists from all parts of the Middle East and North Africa have found their way to Iraq and made common cause with indigenous religious extremists and former members of Saddam's regime.* ***This group cannot be won over and must be defeated – killed or captured – through sustained counterterrorism operations.***

- There are other elements that threaten the democratic process in Iraq, including criminals and Shi'a religious extremists, but we judge that such elements can be handled by Iraqi forces alone and/or assimilated into the political process in the short term.

THE STRATEGY OF OUR ENEMIES

➢ Despite their competing goals, these disparate enemy elements share a common **operational concept:** Intimidate, coerce, or convince the Iraqi public not to support the transition to democracy by persuading them that the nascent Iraqi government is not competent and will be abandoned by a Coalition that lacks the stomach for this fight.

- The enemy's strategy, in short, is to ***intimidate***, ***terrorize***, and ***tear down*** – a strategy with short-term advantage because it is easier to tear down than to build up. But this strategy is not sustainable in the long term because it is rejected by the overwhelming mass of the Iraqi population.

➢ **Enemy Lines of Action.** *The enemy seeks to* ...

- Weaken the Coalition's resolve, and our resolve at home, through barbaric mass-casualty attacks, public slaughter of Iraqi civilians and hostages, infliction of casualties on Coalition forces, and use of the media to spread propaganda and intimidate adversaries.

- Destroy confidence in the Iraqi government by sabotaging key essential service (oil and electricity) nodes and by derailing the political process.

- Damage trust in Iraqi Security Forces through propaganda, infiltration, and barbaric attacks on the weak and the innocent.

- Sabotage Iraqi unity through propaganda against the Shi'a majority punctuated with attacks intended to spark sectarian conflict and civil war.

- Establish safe havens to plan attacks and conduct intimidation campaigns.

- Expand the fight to neighboring states and beyond.

OUR STRATEGY FOR VICTORY IS CLEAR

➢ **Our Strategy is Clear:** We will help the Iraqi people build a new Iraq with a constitutional, representative government that respects civil rights and has security forces sufficient to maintain domestic order and keep Iraq from becoming a safe haven for terrorists. To achieve this end, we are pursuing a comprehensive approach that involves the integrated efforts of the entire United States Government, the Iraqi government, and Coalition governments, and encourages the active involvement of the United Nations, other international organizations, and supportive regional states.

- Our strategy involves **three integrated tracks** – political, security, and economic – each with separate objectives, but together helping Iraqis to defeat the terrorists, Saddamists, and rejectionists, and secure a new democratic state in Iraq.

The Political Track
(Isolate, Engage, Build)

- **Objective:** To help the Iraqi people forge a broadly supported national compact for democratic government, thereby isolating enemy elements from the broader public.

- To achieve this objective, we are helping the Iraqi government:

  ✓ *Isolate* hardened enemy elements from those who can be won over to a peaceful political process by countering false propaganda and demonstrating to the Iraqi people that they have a stake in a viable, democratic Iraq.

  ✓ *Engage* those outside the political process and invite in those willing to turn away from violence through ever-expanding avenues of peaceful participation.

  ✓ *Build* stable, pluralistic, and effective national institutions that can protect the interests of all Iraqis, and facilitate Iraq's full integration into the international community.

The Security Track
(Clear, Hold, Build)

- **Objective:** To develop the Iraqis' capacity to secure their country while carrying out a campaign to defeat the terrorists and neutralize the insurgency.

- To achieve this objective, we are helping the Iraqi government:

  ✓ *Clear* areas of enemy control by remaining on the offensive, killing and capturing enemy fighters and denying them safe-haven.

  ✓ *Hold* areas freed from enemy control by ensuring that they remain under the control of a peaceful Iraqi government with an adequate Iraqi security force presence.

  ✓ *Build* Iraqi Security Forces and the capacity of local institutions to deliver services, advance the rule of law, and nurture civil society.

The Economic Track
(Restore, Reform, Build)

- **Objective:** To assist the Iraqi government in establishing the foundations for a sound economy with the capacity to deliver essential services.

- To achieve this objective, we are helping the Iraqi government:

    ✓ *Restore* Iraq's neglected infrastructure so it can meet increasing demand and the needs of a growing economy.

    ✓ *Reform* Iraq's economy, which has been shaped by war, dictatorship, and sanctions, so that it can be self-sustaining in the future.

    ✓ *Build* the capacity of Iraqi institutions to maintain infrastructure, rejoin the international economic community, and improve the general welfare of all Iraqis.

THIS STRATEGY IS INTEGRATED, AND ITS ELEMENTS ARE MUTUALLY REINFORCING

➢ Progress along one of the political, security, and economic tracks *reinforces progress along the other tracks*. For example:

- As the *political process* has moved forward, terrorists have become more isolated, leading to more intelligence on their leadership and hideouts from Iraqi citizens, which has led to *better security* in previously violent areas, a more stable infrastructure, the prospect of *economic progress*, and expanding *political participation*.

- As *security operations* in Fallujah, Mosul, Tal Afar, and elsewhere have killed or led to the capture of high-level terrorists and insurgents, residents in those areas have come forward to participate in the *political process*, registering and turning out to vote in vast numbers, and providing local residents a meaningful voice in the new Iraq.

- As *economic activities* have progressed, ordinary citizens have returned to normal life and developed a stake in a peaceful Iraq and thus become motivated to support the *political process* and cooperate with *security forces*,

➢ Part II of this paper will discuss the three tracks – political, security, and economic – in more detail, so Americans can better understand the elements of our vital mission, the nature of our strategy, why we believe this strategy will succeed, the progress we are making, and how our government is organized to help Iraqis ensure lasting victory in Iraq.

VICTORY WILL TAKE TIME

➢ **Our Strategy Is Working.** Much has been accomplished in Iraq, including the removal of Saddam's tyranny, negotiation of an interim constitution, restoration of full sovereignty, holding of free national elections, formation of an elected government, drafting of a permanent constitution, ratification of that constitution, introduction of a sound currency, gradual restoration of Iraq's neglected infrastructure, and the ongoing training and equipping of Iraq's security forces.

- **Yet many challenges remain**:

  - Iraq is overcoming decades of a vicious tyranny, under which governmental authority stemmed solely from fear, terror, and brutality. Saddam Hussein devastated Iraq, wrecked its economy, ruined its infrastructure, and destroyed its human capital. It is not realistic to expect a fully functioning democracy, able to defeat its enemies and peacefully reconcile generational grievances, to be in place less than three years after Saddam was finally removed from power.

  - We and the Iraqi people are fighting a ruthless enemy, which is multi-headed, with competing ambitions and differing networks. Getting an accurate picture of this enemy, understanding its makeup and weaknesses, and defeating it, requires patience, persistence, and determined effort along all three strategic tracks.

  - Terrorism and insurgencies historically take many years to defeat, through a combination of political, economic, and military tools. Iraq's violence is different from other such conflicts, where insurgents often had unified command and control or mounted a successful campaign to win the hearts and minds of the population. Nonetheless, Iraq is likely to struggle with some level of violence for many years to come.

  - The neighborhood is inhospitable. Iran and Syria have failed to provide support to Iraq's new government and have in many ways actively undermined it. The region, while including some cooperative actors, has only recently mobilized to support the emergence of a democratic and stable Iraq.

  - The Sunni community is still searching for strong, reliable leadership. Although many Sunnis also suffered under Saddam, leaders from their community generally associated with the Ba'ath Party, not the opposition to the regime. The Sunni religious community, moreover, is less hierarchical and more dispersed, which is reflected in Sunni politics. As a result of these realities, few Sunni leaders have spoken for the larger Sunni community in Iraq. Elections in December will produce elected Sunni leaders who can represent their community with legitimate authority.

  - Many Sunnis are also coming to terms with the reality that their community no longer monopolizes power in Iraq. They are grappling with their role in a democratic country in which they are a minority, albeit with constitutional protections for minority rights and interests.

- Many of Iraq's communities remain skeptical of the central government and nervous about the creation of an Iraqi state where power is concentrated in Baghdad. Their allegiance to a united Iraqi government will depend upon the central government demonstrating the will and capability to govern effectively and fairly on behalf of all Iraqis.

- Earlier efforts to correct past wrongs have sometimes alienated Sunnis who were not complicit with Saddam's crimes. Iraq's leaders need to find a middle ground – between pursuing justice for every past wrong and leaving the past unexamined.

- With democratization has come the emergence of new groups, not all of whom have shared the goal of a free, pluralistic, and democratic Iraq. Some groups – like members of the Mahdi Militia – have sought to maximize discontent with the Coalition presence and have at times clashed violently with other parties.

- The continued existence and influence of militias and armed groups, often affiliated with political parties, hamper the rule of law in some parts of Iraq. These groups have also infiltrated the police forces and sparked violent exchanges in areas of the country that are otherwise peaceful.

- Iraq's economy is still shackled with many vestiges of a highly centralized economy and stagnant and corrupt institutions. Creating new institutions, reforming old ones, and developing new policies will be necessary to encourage economic growth. The prosperity of average Iraqis will be enhanced only if Iraq reduces the massive subsidy programs that burden its economy.

WHY OUR STRATEGY IS (AND MUST BE) CONDITIONS-BASED

➤ Success in the short, medium, and long run will depend on progress in overcoming these challenges and on the *conditions on the ground in Iraq*. Our strategy – along the political, security, and economic tracks – is establishing the conditions for victory. These conditions include:

- Progress in the Iraqi political process and the increasing willingness of Iraqis to forge political compromises;

- Consolidation of gains in the training of Iraqi Security Forces (ISF);

- Commitment to and implementation of economic reforms by Iraqi leaders;

- Increased cooperation of Iraq's neighbors;

- Expanded support from the international community;

- Continued support of the American people.

- Although we are confident of victory in Iraq, *we will not put a date certain on when each stage of success will be reached* – because the timing of success depends upon meeting certain conditions, not arbitrary timetables.

  - Arbitrary deadlines or timetables for withdrawal of Coalition forces – divorced from conditions on the ground – would be **irresponsible and deadly**, as they would suggest to the terrorists, Saddamists, and rejectionists that they can simply wait to win.

  - **No war has ever been won on a timetable – and neither will this one.**

- Lack of a timetable, however, does not mean that the Coalition's posture in Iraq (both military and political) is static. On the contrary, *we continually adjust our posture and approaches as conditions evolve and Iraqi capabilities grow*.

  - Coalition troop levels, for example, will **increase** where necessary to defeat the enemy or provide additional security for key events like the referendum and elections. But troop levels will **decrease** over time, as Iraqis continue to take on more of the security and civilian responsibilities themselves.

  - We expect, but cannot guarantee, that our force posture will change over the next year, as the political process consolidates and as Iraqi Security Forces grow and gain experience.

    - ✓ As Iraqis take on more responsibility for security, Coalition forces will increasingly move to supporting roles in most areas. The mission of our forces will change – from conducting operations and keeping the peace, to more specialized operations targeted at the most vicious terrorists and leadership networks.

    - ✓ As security conditions improve and as Iraqi Security Forces become increasingly capable of securing their own country, our forces will increasingly move out of the cities, reduce the number of bases from which we operate, and conduct fewer patrols and convoy missions.

    - ✓ While our military presence may become less visible, it will remain lethal and decisive, able to confront the enemy wherever it may gather and organize.

  - As our posture changes over time, so too will the posture of our Coalition partners. We and the Iraqis must work with them to coordinate our efforts, helping Iraq to consolidate and secure its gains on many different fronts.

OUR STRATEGY TRACKS AND MEASURES PROGRESS

- We track numerous indicators to map the progress of our strategy and change our tactics whenever necessary. Detailed reports – both classified and unclassified – are issued weekly, monthly, and quarterly by relevant agencies and military units.

  - Many of these reports with detailed metrics are released to the public, and are readily accessible. For example:

- Gains in training Iraqi security forces are updated weekly at www.mnstci.iraq.centcom.mil;

- Improvements in the economy and infrastructure are collected weekly by the State Department (www.state.gov/p/nea/rls/rpt/iraqstatus/) as well as USAID, which continually updates its many ongoing programs and initiatives in Iraq (www.usaid.gov/iraq);

- Extensive reports are also made every three months to Congress, and are accessible at the State (www.state.gov/p/nea/rls/rpt/2207/) and Defense (www.defenselink.mil/pubs/) Department websites.

  ✓ Americans can read and assess these reports to get a better sense of what is being done in Iraq and the progress being made on a daily, weekly, and monthly basis.

- Some of the most important metrics we track are:

  - **Political**: The political benchmarks set forth in U.N. Security Council Resolution 1546 and the Transitional Administrative Law; the number of Iraqis from all areas willing to participate in the political process as evidenced by voter registration and turnout.

  - **Security**: The quantity and quality of Iraqi units; the number of actionable intelligence tips received from Iraqis; the percentage of operations conducted by Iraqis alone or with minor Coalition assistance; the number of car bombs intercepted and defused; offensive operations conducted by Iraqi and Coalition forces; and the number of contacts initiated by Coalition forces, as opposed to the enemy.

  - **Economic**: GDP; per capita GDP; inflation; electricity generated and delivered; barrels of oil produced and exported; and numbers of businesses opened.

- Other indicators are also important to success, but less subject to precise measurement, such as the extent to which principles of transparency, trust in government institutions, and acceptance of the rule of law are taking hold amongst a population that has never known them.

- These indicators **have more strategic significance** than the metrics that the terrorists and insurgents want the world to use as a measure of progress or failure: number of bombings.

  ➢ The following pages break down the three tracks of our strategy – political, security, economic – and explain the logic behind them in more detail.

"The only way our enemies can succeed is if we forget the lessons of September the 11th, if we abandon the Iraqi people to men like Zarqawi, and if we yield the future of the Middle East to men like Bin Laden. For the sake of our nation's security, this will not happen on my watch."

– President George W. Bush, June 28, 2005

OUR NATIONAL STRATEGY FOR VICTORY IN IRAQ:
Helping the Iraqi People Defeat the Terrorists and Build an Inclusive Democratic State

PART II – STRATEGY IN DETAIL

"America's task in Iraq is not only to defeat an enemy, it is to give strength to a friend – a free, representative government that serves its people and fights on their behalf."

– President George W. Bush, May 24, 2004

THE POLITICAL TRACK IN DETAIL

Strategic Summary: *Isolate, Engage, Build*

➤ The political track of our strategy is based on **six core assumptions**:

- **First,** like people in all parts of the world, from all cultures and religions, when given the opportunity, the Iraqi people prefer to live in freedom rather than under tyranny.

- **Second**, a critical mass of Iraqis in all areas of the country will not embrace the perverse vision offered by the terrorists. Most rejectionists can over time be persuaded to no longer seek the privileges of dictatorship – and in exchange will embrace the rewards of democratic stability.

- **Third**, an enduring democracy is not built through elections alone: critical components include transparent, effective institutions and a national constitutional compact.

- **Fourth**, federalism is not a precursor to the breakup of Iraq, but instead is a prerequisite for a united country and better governance. Federalism allows a strong central government to exercise the powers of a sovereign state, while enabling regional bodies to make decisions that protect the interests of local populations.

- **Fifth**, it is in the fundamental interests of all Iraqi communities – and of the region – that Iraq stays a united country. This shared objective creates space for compromise across ethnic and religious divides and for the steady growth of national institutions.

- **Sixth**, Iraq needs and can receive the support of the region and the international community to solidify its successes.

STRATEGIC LOGIC BEHIND THE POLITICAL TRACK

➤ Our efforts and those of the Iraqis on the political track are geared toward *isolating* hard-core rejectionists by expanding avenues for political participation at all levels of government, *engaging* the region and all Iraqi communities to demonstrate that there is a place for all groups in the new Iraq, and *building* national Iraqi institutions and international support to advance the rule of law and offer the Iraqi people a solid framework for a better and more peaceful future.

- How will this help the Iraqis – with Coalition support – defeat the enemy and achieve our larger goals?

  - Progress in the political process – meeting political benchmarks – will provide momentum against the insurgency and indicate to people "on the fence" that the old regime has passed and that the effort to build a new Iraq will succeed.

  - Inclusive institutions that offer power-sharing mechanisms and minority protections will demonstrate to disaffected Sunnis that they have influence and the ability to protect their interests in a democratic Iraq.

  - Commitment to democracy – rather than other forms of governance – not only is consistent with our values, but is essential to keeping the long-oppressed Shi'a and Kurds as our partners in Iraq.

  - Increasingly robust Iraqi political institutions expose the falsity of enemy propaganda that Iraq is "under occupation," with decisions being made by non-Iraqis. Such institutions also provide peaceful means for reconciliation and bridging divides.

  - Due to the historical, cultural, political, and economic links between Iraq and its neighbors, many surrounding countries can help Iraq secure its borders and encourage Sunni rejectionists to renounce violence and enter the political process.

  - Expanding international support for Iraq will demonstrate to Iraqis and the world that Iraq is a valuable member of the international community and will further broaden the political and economic support provided to Iraq.

PROGRESS ON THE POLITICAL TRACK

➤ Our *Isolate, Engage, and Build* strategy is working: Iraqis have hit every political benchmark in their transitional political process – and are on track to hit the next one: elections in December to select a four-year government under a democratic constitution, with full participation from all of Iraq's main ethnic and religious communities.

- In January, 8.5 million Iraqis defied terrorist threats to vote for Iraq's first freely elected national government and provincial governments.

- In April, the elected leaders of Iraq's national legislature came together to form a diverse cabinet that represented all groups, despite election results that heavily favored the Shi'a and Kurdish communities.

- In June, the national legislature formally invited non-elected Sunni Arab leaders to join constitutional negotiations, demonstrating that leaders from all communities understood the importance of a constitution with input from Iraq's major groups.

- In summer/autumn 2005, Iraq's elected national legislature – and the Sunni leaders invited to join the process – drafted a constitution that was a huge step for Iraq and the region. This draft constitution invests the sovereignty of Iraq in the people and their right to vote, protects individual rights and religious freedoms, and puts forward sophisticated institutional arrangements to safeguard minority rights.

- By the end of September 2005, approximately one million new voters came forward to check their names on Iraq's voting rolls – the vast majority in Sunni areas. In October, nearly 10 million Iraqis from all areas of the country again defied terrorist threats to vote in the constitutional referendum. The constitution was ratified.

- Interest in the political process is stronger than ever. More than 300 parties and coalitions are registered for the December elections, and even those who opposed the constitution have organized for the December vote.

- In a strategic shift, Sunnis are turning to the political process to advance their interests. During the constitutional referendum, turnout in Sunni areas was strong. Although many Sunnis voted against the constitution, amendments made days before the referendum in response to Sunni requests will permit further changes after the new government is established. This and other provisions of the constitution that defer important issues to the new assembly will ensure that elected Sunni leaders are able to influence the shape of the Iraqi state.

- A recent change in the electoral process also provides all Iraqis a place in the new assembly. In the January 2005 election, representation in the assembly was directly related to turnout, which led to the depressed Sunni numbers in the body. Today's electoral system allocates representation by province, which guarantees that even if communities go to the polls in varying strengths, they will all have representation in the new assembly.

- Signs of a vibrant political life are sprouting. The constitutional drafting committee received more than 500,000 public comments on various provisions. More than 100 newspapers freely discuss political events every day in Iraq. Campaign posters are displayed openly and in increasing number in most of Iraq's major cities.

➢ As Iraq's political institutions mature, its judicial system has become an independent branch, better able to promote the rule of law:

- Iraq's judiciary is organized by an independent council of judges, as in most civil law countries. Saddam Hussein's system of "secret courts" has been abolished.

- One year ago, the Central Criminal Court of Iraq had capacity to prosecute fewer than 10 trials and investigative hearings per month. In the first two weeks of September 2005 alone, the Court prosecuted more than 50 multi-defendant trials, and conducted over 100 investigative hearings. The Court is now expanding its reach throughout Iraq with separate branches in local provinces.

- Hundreds of judges have been trained since the fall of Saddam Hussein. These judges are now working and resolving cases under Iraqi law. In 2003, approximately 4,000 felony cases were resolved in Iraqi courts. In 2004, they resolved more than twice that number. This year, Iraqi courts are on track to resolve more than 10,000 felony cases.

➤ International support for Iraq's political development is also growing:

- The United Nations Security Council has enacted a series of unanimous resolutions that authorize the presence of Coalition forces and anchor the Iraqi political process with international backing. In November, the United Nations Security Council passed resolution 1637, which – at the request of the Iraqi government – unanimously extended authorization for the Coalition forces to operate in Iraq.

- The United Nations is also playing an important role in Iraq's political transition, and plans to expand its capacity with hundreds of personnel located throughout the country. The Arab League, the European Union, and other important regional actors are all engaged and working to support the Iraqi political process.

- Iraq is winning wider support from its fellow Arab states as well. In November, the Arab League hosted a meeting in Cairo to promote Iraqi national reconciliation and the political process; Iraqi leaders are being received by Arab heads of state; and many Arab countries publicly supported Iraq's constitutional referendum and called for the broad participation of all Iraqis in Iraq's political process.

- At the same time, change is coming to the region, with Syrian occupation ended and democracy emerging in Lebanon, and free elections and new leadership in the Palestinian Territories. From Kuwait to Morocco, Jordan, and Egypt, there are stirrings of political pluralism, often for the first time in generations.

CONTINUED CHALLENGES IN THE POLITICAL SPHERE

➤ Even with this solid progress, we and our Iraqi partners continue to face multiple challenges in the political sphere, including:

- Ensuring that those who join the political process leave behind violence entirely;

- Building national institutions when past divisions and current suspicions have led many Iraqis to look to regional or sectarian bodies to protect their interests;

- Nurturing a culture of reconciliation, human rights, and transparency in a society scarred by three decades of arbitrary violence and rampant corruption;

- Building political movements based on issues and platforms, instead of identity;

- Encouraging cooperation across ethnic, religious and tribal divides when many wounds are still fresh and have been exacerbated by recent hardships;

- Convincing all regional states to welcome and actively support the new Iraqi state politically and financially;

- Building ministerial capacity to advance effective government and reduce corruption.

THE SECURITY TRACK IN DETAIL

Strategic Summary: *Clear, Hold, Build*

➤ The security track is based on **six core** assumptions:

- **First**, the terrorists, Saddamists, and rejectionists do not have the manpower or firepower to achieve a military victory over the Coalition and Iraqi Security Forces. They can win only if we surrender.

- **Second**, our own political will is steadfast and will allow America to keep troops in Iraq – to fight terrorists while training and mentoring Iraqi forces – until the mission is done, increasing or decreasing troop levels only as conditions warrant.

- **Third**, progress on the political front will improve the intelligence picture by helping distinguish those who can be won over to support the new Iraqi state from the terrorists and insurgents who must either be killed or captured, detained, and prosecuted.

- **Fourth**, the training, equipping, and mentoring of Iraqi Security Forces will produce an army and police force capable of independently providing security and maintaining public order in Iraq.

- **Fifth**, regional meddling and infiltrations can be contained and/or neutralized.

- **Sixth**, while we can help, assist, and train, Iraqis will ultimately be the ones to eliminate their security threats over the long term.

STRATEGIC LOGIC BEHIND SECURITY TRACK

➤ *We are helping the Iraqi Security Forces and the Iraqi government take territory out of enemy control (**clear**); keep and consolidate the influence of the Iraqi government afterwards (**hold**); and establish new local institutions that advance civil society and the rule of law in areas formerly under enemy influence and control (**build**).*

- Efforts on the security track include offensive operations against the enemy, protection of key communication and infrastructure nodes, post-conflict stabilization operations, and the training, equipping, and mentoring of Iraqi Security Forces. Coalition transition teams are embedded in all Iraqi Army battalions to provide assistance and guidance when needed.

➤ The model that works is clear – it is resource intensive, requires commitment and resolve, and involves tools across the civilian and military spectrum, including:

- The right balance of Coalition and Iraqi forces conducting offensive operations;

- Preparation for such operations through contact and negotiation between local and federal Iraqi government officials;

- Adequate Iraqi forces to provide security for the population and guard against future intimidation;

- Cooperation with and support for local institutions to govern after Coalition forces leave;

- Prompt disbursal of aid for quick and visible reconstruction;

- Central government authorities who pay attention to local needs.

➤ How will this help the Iraqis – with Coalition support – defeat the enemy and achieve our larger goals?

- Offensive operations disrupt enemy networks and deprive enemy elements of safe havens from which they can rest, train, rearm, and plan attacks against the Coalition, the Iraqi government, and Iraqi civilians.

- Localized post-conflict operations – providing security, economic assistance, and support to civilian institutions in newly cleared areas – further isolate enemy elements from the rest of the population and give Iraqis space to participate in a peaceful political process.

- Infrastructure protection helps ensure that the Iraqi government can collect revenues and provide basic services to the people, which is critical to building confidence in the government and weaning support away from insurgents.

- Putting capable Iraqis forward in the fight increases the overall effectiveness of U.S.-Iraqi operations, as Iraqis are better able to collect intelligence and identify threats in their neighborhoods.

- As Iraqi forces become more and more capable, our military posture will shift, leaving Coalition forces increasingly focused on specialized counter-terrorism missions to hunt, capture, and kill terrorist leaders and break up their funding and resource networks.

PROGRESS ON THE SECURITY TRACK

➢ Our *clear*, *hold*, and *build* strategy is working:

- *Significant progress has been made in wresting territory from enemy control*. During much of 2004, major parts of Iraq and important urban centers were no-go areas for Iraqi and Coalition forces. Fallujah, Najaf, and Samara were under enemy control. Today, these cities are under Iraqi government control, and the political process is taking hold. Outside of major urban areas, Iraqi and Coalition forces are clearing out hard core enemy elements, maintaining a security presence, and building local institutions to advance local reconstruction and civil society.

- *Actionable intelligence is improving*. Due to greater confidence in the Iraqi state and growing frustration with the terrorists, Saddamists, and rejectionists, Iraqi citizens are providing more intelligence to Iraqis and Coalition forces. In March 2005, Iraqi and Coalition forces received more than 400 intelligence tips from Iraqi citizens; in August, they received 3,300, and in September more than 4,700.

- *Iraqi forces are growing in number*. As of November 2005, there were more than 212,000 trained and equipped Iraqi Security Forces, compared with 96,000 in September of last year. In August 2004, there were five Iraqi army battalions in the fight; now more than 120 Iraqi army and police battalions are in the fight. Of these battalions, more than 80 are fighting side-by-side with Coalition forces and more than 40 others are taking the lead in the fight. More battalions are being recruited, trained, and fielded. In July 2004 there were no operational Iraqi brigade or division headquarters; now there are seven division and more than 30 brigade headquarters in the Iraqi army. In June 2004, there were no Iraqi combat support or service support battalions; now there are a half dozen operational battalions supporting fielded Iraqi units.

- *Iraqi forces are growing in capability*. In June 2004, no Iraqi Security Force unit controlled territory. The Coalition provided most of the security in Iraq. Today, much of Baghdad province is under the control of Iraqi forces, the cities of Najaf and Karbala are controlled by Iraqi forces, and other Iraqi battalions and brigades control hundreds of square miles of territory in other Iraqi provinces. A year ago, the Iraqi Air Force had no aircraft; today its three operational squadrons provide airlift and reconnaissance support and Iraqi pilots are training on newly arrived helicopters. A year ago during the operation to liberate Fallujah, five Iraqi battalions took part in the fight. For the most part, they fell in behind Coalition forces to help control territory already seized by Coalition units. No Iraqi units controlled their own battle space. In September 2005, during Operation Restoring Rights in Tal Afar, eleven Iraqi battalions participated, controlling their own battle space, and outnumbering Coalition forces for the first time in a major offensive operation. Over the last six months, the number of patrols being conducted independently by Iraqi forces has doubled, bringing the overall percentage to nearly a quarter of all patrols in theater.

- *Iraqis are committed to building up their security establishment*. Despite repeated and brutal attacks against Iraqi Security Forces, volunteers continue to outpace an already substantial demand. In the past several months alone, nearly 5,000 recruits have joined from Sunni areas. In the recently cleared Tal Afar, more than 200 local volunteers have begun police training before returning to help protect their city. In Anbar, Sunnis have lined up to join the Iraqi army and police, planning to return to their home province and help protect it from terrorists.

- ***Iraqis are taking on specialized missions central to overall success.*** Four Strategic Infrastructure Battalions, with more than 3,000 personnel, have completed training and will soon assume the specific mission of guarding vital infrastructure nodes from terrorist attack. A Special Police Unit highly trained for hostage rescue has almost 200 operators and is conducting operations almost every week in Baghdad and Mosul. In the past several months, hundreds of Iraqi soldiers have undergone intensive special operations training and are now in the fight, hunting, killing, and capturing the most-wanted terrorist leaders.

- ***Iraq is building an officer corps that will be loyal to the Iraqi government, not a particular group or tribe.*** The Iraqi army now has three officer academies training the next generation of junior officers for its army. In September, NATO inaugurated a new military staff college in Baghdad that will eventually train more than 1,000 senior Iraqi officers each year. Today, however, the vast majority of Iraqi police and army recruits are being taught by Iraqi instructors. By training the trainers, we are creating an institutional capability that will allow the Iraqi forces to continue to develop and grow long after Coalition forces have left Iraq.

CONTINUED CHALLENGES IN THE SECURITY SPHERE

➢ Even with this progress, we and our Iraqi partners continue to face multiple challenges in the security sphere, including:

- Countering the intimidation and brutality of enemies whose tactics are not constrained by law or moral norms;

- Building representative Iraqi security forces and institutions while guarding against infiltration by elements whose first loyalties are to persons or institutions other than the Iraqi government;

- Neutralizing the actions of countries like Syria and Iran, which provide comfort and/or support to terrorists and the enemies of democracy in Iraq;

- Refining our understanding of the constantly changing nature of, and relationships between, terrorist groups, other enemy elements, and their networks;

- Addressing the militias and armed groups that are outside the formal security sector and central government command;

- Ensuring that the security ministries – as well as the fighting forces – have the capacity to sustain Iraq's new army;

- Integrating political, economic, and security tools – and synchronizing them with Iraqi government efforts – to provide the best post-conflict operations possible.

"My aim is 100 percent clear: all the terrorists living here, they go now. Saddam . . . it's finished. He's broken. Now is the new Iraq."

-Gen. Muhammad al-Sumraa, Iraq 303rd Battalion,
Haifa Street, Baghdad, August 14, 2005

THE ECONOMIC TRACK IN DETAIL

Strategic Summary: *Restore, Reform, Build*

➢ The economic track is based on **six core assumptions**:

- **First**, Iraq has the potential to be not just viable, but prosperous and self-sustaining.

- **Second**, a free and prosperous Iraq is in the economic interest of everybody, including Iraq's neighbors and the greater Middle East. A flourishing Iraq can spur economic activity and reform in one of the world's most vital regions.

- **Third**, increased economic opportunity in Iraq and a growing economy will give larger numbers of Iraqis an economic stake in a peaceful country, and drain the influence of radicals and rejectionists who recruit the unemployed and thrive on resentment.

- **Fourth**, economic change in Iraq will be steady but gradual given a generation of neglect, corrosive misrule, and central planning that stifled entrepreneurship and initiative.

- **Fifth**, Iraq can be a reliable and contributing partner in the international economic community, demonstrating the fruits of good governance and transparency.

- **Sixth**, Iraq will need financial support from the region and international community as its economy transitions from being guided by command principles and hampered by poor infrastructure to a more self-sustaining posture.

STRATEGIC LOGIC BEHIND THE ECONOMIC TRACK

➢ Our efforts have focused on helping Iraq restore its neglected infrastructure so it can provide essential services to the population while encouraging economic reforms, greater transparency, and accountability in the economic realm. The international community has been instrumental in these efforts, but there is room for the international community to do more. Foreign direct investment, over time, will play an increasing role in fueling Iraq's economic growth.

- How will these efforts help the Iraqis – with Coalition support – defeat the enemy and achieve our larger goals?

- The rebuilding of Iraq's infrastructure and the provision of essential services will **increase the confidence of Iraqis** in their government and help convince them that the government is offering them a brighter future. People will then be more likely to cooperate with the government, and provide intelligence against the enemy, creating a less hospitable environment for the terrorists and insurgents.

- Efforts in the reconstruction realm have **significant implications in the security realm** when they focus on rebuilding post-conflict cities and towns. Compensation for civilians hurt by counterterrorism operations and the restoration of some economic vibrancy to areas formerly under terrorist control can help ease resentment and win over an otherwise suspicious population.

- Economic growth and reform of Saddam-era laws and regulations will be critical to ensuring that **Iraq can support and maintain** the new security institutions that the country is developing, attract new investment to Iraq, and become a full, integrated member of the international economic community.

- Economic growth and market reform – and the promotion of Iraq's private sector – are necessary to **expand job opportunities** for the youthful Iraqi population and decrease unemployment that makes some Iraqis more vulnerable to terrorist or insurgent recruiting.

PROGRESS ON THE ECONOMIC TRACK

➤ Our *restore*, *reform*, *build*, strategy is achieving results:

- Oil production increased from an average of 1.58 million barrels per day in 2003, to an average of 2.25 million barrels per day in 2004. Iraq presently is producing on average 2.1 million barrels per day, a slight decrease due to terrorist attacks on infrastructure, dilapidated and insufficient infrastructure, and poor maintenance practices. We are helping the Iraqis address each challenge so the country can have a dependable income stream.

- Iraq's nominal GDP recovered from its nadir of $13.6 billion in 2003 to $25.5 billion in 2004, led primarily by the recovery of the oil sector. According to the International Monetary Fund, GDP is expected to grow in real terms by 3.7 percent in 2005 and nearly 17 percent in 2006.

- Iraq's exchange rate has been stable since the introduction of its new currency in 2004 and remains so at approximately 1,475 Iraqi Dinar/$1. A stable currency has allowed the Central Bank of Iraq to better manage inflationary pressures.

- According to the IMF, per capita GDP, an important measure of poverty, rebounded to $942 in 2004 (after dropping to $518 in 2003), and is expected to continue to increase to over $1,000 in 2005.

- Since April 2003, Iraq has registered more than 30,000 new businesses, and its stock market (established in April 2004) currently lists nearly 90 companies with an average daily trading volume over $100 million (from January to May 2005), up from an average of $86 million in 2004.

- Iraq is rejoining the international financial community: it is on the road to WTO accession, has completed its first IMF economic health report card in 25 years, and secured an agreement that could lead to as much as 80 percent reduction from the Paris Club for Saddam-era debt.

- At the October 2003 Madrid International Donors Conference, donors other than the United States pledged over $13 billion in assistance for the reconstruction of Iraq, including $8 billion from foreign governments and $5.5 billion in lending from the World Bank and International Monetary Fund, to be disbursed from 2004 through 2007.

- Iraqi business leaders are decidedly optimistic about the growth of the economy as well as the growth of their own businesses.

  - *According to a September poll by Zogby International for the Center for International Private Enterprise, **77 percent** of Iraqi businesses anticipate growth in the national economy over the next two years and **69 percent** of respondents describe themselves as being "**optimistic**" about Iraq's economic future.*

- Today in Iraq there are more than 3 million cell phone subscribers. In 2003 there were virtually none.

CONTINUED CHALLENGES IN THE ECONOMIC SPHERE

➢ Even with this progress, Iraq continues to face multiple challenges in the economic sphere, including:

- Facilitating investment in Iraq's oil sector to increase production from the current 2.1 million barrels per day to more than 5 million per day;

- Overcoming decades of Saddam's neglect of Iraq's basic infrastructure;

- Preventing, repairing, and overcoming terrorist and insurgent attacks against vital infrastructure, especially electricity and oil related nodes;

- Dealing with an increased demand for electricity;

  - The liberalization of border trade and increased salaries of Iraqis, has led to increased demand for electrical goods since 2003, which has driven up demand for electricity. At the same time, insurgent attacks and dilapidated infrastructure have complicated efforts to bring more electricity on-line. The Iraqis, with our assistance, are working to ease electricity constraints by providing greater security to transmission lines, investing in new generation capacity, and evaluating the prospects of using natural gas – as opposed to inefficient fuels – to keep generators running.

- Creating a payment system and a banking infrastructure that are responsive to the needs of the domestic and international communities, and that allow transactions involving possible money laundering, terrorist financing and other financial crimes to be detected;

- Balancing the need for economic reform – particularly of bloated fuel and food subsidies – with political realities;

- Building the administrative and technical capacities of Iraqi ministries;

- Ensuring as much reconstruction assistance as possible flows to Iraqi entities (ministries and businesses);

- Encouraging local and regional capacity building after decades of a highly centralized government, so that reconstruction and essential services can be more evenly distributed throughout Iraq;

- Facilitating progress toward a market-oriented economy by reforming commercial laws and other bureaucratic obstacles to attract investment and private sector involvement;

- Encouraging many in the region and the international community to disburse their pledges more quickly and contribute even greater resources to Iraq's reconstruction.

ORGANIZATION FOR VICTORY

The 8 Strategic Pillars

- Our strategy for victory along the political, security, and economic tracks incorporates **every aspect of American power**, with assistance from agencies throughout the federal government, and the involvement of the United Nations, other international organizations, Coalition countries, and other supportive countries and regional states. *It is predicated on the belief that we must marshal these resources to help Iraqis overcome the challenges remaining before them.*

  - Our strategy is **comprehensive**, and relies on a sustained and courageous effort by hundreds of thousands of Americans and Coalition partners, military and civilian, in the security, political, economic, and diplomatic realms – in addition to the millions of Iraqis they work with everyday.

  - To organize these efforts, we have broken down our political/security/economic strategy into **eight pillars** or strategic objectives:

    1. Defeat the Terrorists and Neutralize the Insurgency
    2. Transition Iraq to Security Self-Reliance
    3. Help Iraqis Form a National Compact for Democratic Government
    4. Help Iraq Build Government Capacity and Provide Essential Services
    5. Help Iraq Strengthen its Economy
    6. Help Iraq Strengthen the Rule of Law and Promote Civil Rights

7. Increase International Support for Iraq
8. Strengthen Public Understanding of Coalition Efforts and Public Isolation of the Insurgents

➢ Each Strategic Pillar contains at least five independent lines of action and scores of sub-actions, with specific objectives being met by military and civilian volunteers, Iraqis, and our international partners.

- Underlying each line of action is a series of missions and tasks assigned to military and civilian units in Iraq. These missions and tasks are largely classified, but we seek to characterize them in the unclassified appendix that follows. By understanding our organization, Americans can better understand our strategy and the steps we are taking to achieve long-term victory in Iraq.

  ✓ Each pillar has a corresponding interagency working group – where professionals from the National Security Council, State Department, Defense Department, Treasury Department, Commerce Department, Homeland Security, and other agencies coordinate policy, review and assess the progress that is being made, develop new proposals for action whenever necessary, and oversee the implementation of existing policies.

- Weekly strategy sessions at senior levels of the United States Government ensure that Iraq remains a **top priority** for all relevant agencies with actions along all the eight pillars of activity integrated and calibrated to changed circumstances whenever necessary.

  ✓ *This is the essence of a conditions-based strategy: constantly reviewing conditions as they evolve and changing and redirecting tactics as needed to keep a trajectory towards long-term success.*

- Our team in Baghdad – led by Ambassador Zalmay Khalilzad and General George Casey – works to implement policy on the ground and lay the foundation for long-term success.

➢ The following appendix outlines each Pillar to provide a sense of how our mission in Iraq is organized. As these pages demonstrate, there is hard work to do, but the stakes could not be higher, and *we are organized for victory to an extent not seen since the end of the Cold War.*

"There's always a temptation, in the middle of a long struggle, to seek the quiet life, to escape the duties and problems of the world, and to hope the enemy grows weary of fanaticism and tired of murder. This would be a pleasant world, but it's not the world we live in. The enemy is never tired, never sated, never content with yesterday's brutality. This enemy considers every retreat of the civilized world as an invitation to greater violence. In Iraq, there is no peace without victory. We will keep our nerve, and we will win that victory."

-President George W. Bush, October 6, 2005

APPENDIX

The Eight Pillars

Defeat the Terrorists and Neutralize the Insurgency

STRATEGIC OBJECTIVE: Iraq is not a source of terrorists or terrorist resources, and neither terrorists, Saddamists, nor rejectionists are able to prevent Iraq's political and economic progress. They cannot stop the Iraqi government's development of a constitutional representative democracy, the provision of essential services, a market economy that provides goods, services, and employment for Iraqis, or the free flow of information and ideas.

Status: Increasingly capable Iraqi security forces are working with Coalition forces to disrupt enemy operations by preventing the establishment of enemy safe havens in Iraq and by providing enhanced protection of key infrastructure. They are disrupting enemy movements across borders and are applying pressure to stop the use of Syrian territory to facilitate terrorist activities in Iraq. As the Iraqi government establishes its authority, it generates – with international assistance – programs and projects to benefit the Iraqi people and isolate violent extremists from the population. As security improves, the United States will work with Iraqi authorities to strengthen provincial governments, especially through the use of project funding.

The United States is helping Iraq achieve this objective by pursuing the following lines of action:

- Staying on the offensive by aiding the Iraqi government to eliminate enemy safe havens and hunt down members of terrorist cells and key enemy leaders

- Facilitating the establishment of effective local governance and security elements to ensure post-conflict stability and security

- Assisting Iraqi authorities to suppress foreign fighter infiltration and denying terrorists freedom of movement

- Working with the Iraqi government to disrupt enemy financial networks

- Helping the Iraqis to harden, build redundancy, and protect critical infrastructure

"To be sure, the terrorists and insurgents are out to shake our will. But they will not succeed. The Iraqi people, enabled by the military and civilian members of the coalition, will succeed."

-General George Casey, Commander, US Forces in Iraq, June 2005

Transition Iraq to Security Self-Reliance

STRATEGIC OBJECTIVE: The Government of Iraq provides for the internal security of Iraq, monitors and controls its borders, successfully defends against terrorists and other security threats.

Status: Iraqi security forces, both military and police, are growing in capability through regular and challenging training. They are gaining operational experience to bring the fight directly to the enemies of democracy in Iraq. As Iraqi units become more capable, they are moving from fighting alongside Coalition forces, to taking the lead in operations against the enemy. As more units gain experience and grow more capable, Iraqis will take the lead in the bulk of operations, and Coalition forces will increasingly focus on specialized missions, such as killing or capturing Zarqawi and his henchmen.

The United States is helping Iraq achieve this objective by pursuing the following lines of action:

- Helping to train and equip the Iraqi Security Forces, military, and police, so they can combat terrorist and other enemy activity and maintain a secure environment in Iraq

- Assisting in the development of Iraq's security ministries to control, manage, and sustain the Iraqi security forces and assume greater responsibility for the security of the state

- Increasing the Iraqi government's capability to protect its key economic infrastructure, control its borders, and deny entry to foreign fighters and violent extremists

- Improving the Iraqi government's intelligence capability to augment security force efforts and to protect national interests

"The principal task of our military is to find and defeat the terrorists, and that is why we are on the offense. And as we pursue the terrorists, our military is helping to train Iraqi security forces so that they can defend their people and fight the enemy on their own."

-President George W. Bush, June 28, 2005

Help Iraqis Forge a National Compact for Democratic Government

STRATEGIC OBJECTIVE: Iraq evolves into a free, federal, democratic, pluralist, and unified state representative of all Iraqi citizens.

<u>Status</u>: A generation of arbitrary and vicious rule by Saddam Hussein corrupted Iraq's public life and left most Iraqis with little trust in government institutions. Iraqis are now working to overcome this legacy, but their scarred history and rich diversity of religion, ethnicity, language, and experience requires sophisticated political arrangements to ensure that all Iraqis have a place in the new Iraq. The continuation of the political process, coupled with the emergence of compromises across ethnic and religious divides, is drawing in more and more Iraqis, including those who have only known violence as the final arbiter of any dispute.

<u>**The United States is helping Iraq achieve this objective through the following lines of action**</u>:

- Supporting Iraqi leaders in their quest to bring all Iraqis into the political process, through dialogue and the creation of inclusive institutions

- Offering advice and technical support on elections and effective governance

- Helping to build national institutions that transcend regional and sectarian interests

- Helping the Iraqis replace the corrupt and centralized system of Saddam's regime with effective government bodies at the local, provincial, and national levels

- Assisting with the design and implementation of civic outreach and education programs to help Iraqi citizens understand their rights and responsibilities in a democratic system

- Promoting transparency in the executive, legislative, and judicial branches of government

- Supporting efforts by the Iraqi Transitional Government and successor governments to develop effective and legitimate institutions for legislation, law enforcement, the administration of justice, and the equitable administration of all public services

"This constitution is a national compact between the communities of Iraq, to have a roadmap for the future so they can live together in mutual respect and mutual tolerance. And that's why it's so important and . . . at the same time why it's so difficult."

-Ambassador to Iraq Zalmay Khalilzad, August 2005

Help Iraq Build Government Capacity and Provide Essential Services

STRATEGIC OBJECTIVE: The Iraqi government is able to provide essential services to the population of Iraq.

Status: Saddam Hussein pillaged Iraq's infrastructure and directed essential services to favored areas populated with Ba'ath party loyalists. This legacy is now further complicated by forces in Iraq that deliberately target civilian infrastructure to dishearten the public and weaken the central government. These strains on Iraq's infrastructure are exacerbated by an ever-growing demand for electricity and fuel (resulting from an upward spiral of demand for new cars, generators, and air conditioners) and subsidies that make prices for power among the lowest in the world. These difficulties, among others, help explain why progress in these areas has not been as robust as some expected. Nevertheless, impressive gains are being made, with new schools and clinics opening and water projects and electricity generation coming on line.

The United States is helping Iraq achieve this objective through the following lines of action:

- Rehabilitating critical infrastructure in the production and distribution of fuels and electric power as well as training engineers to maintain and operate this infrastructure

- Supporting and strengthening the nascent institutions of public utilities and regulatory agencies

- Rehabilitating water and sanitation infrastructure to provide safe drinking water and reducing the transmission of water-borne disease

- Building and rehabilitating health care facilities, with a focus on impoverished neighborhoods and communities

- Rehabilitating schools, providing new textbooks, computers and materials, and training teachers and school administrative staff

- Encouraging international donors to expand infrastructure and capacity-building efforts through prompt disbursement of pledges

"As to the situation with infrastructure and services for Iraq, the United States, of course, has devoted $18.6 billion to reconstruction in Iraq, a good bit of that to water projects, to electricity. I think it's awfully important to step back and recognize that under Saddam Hussein this Iraqi infrastructure was seriously deteriorated. ... There is already a lot of work that has gone on on electricity, a lot of work that has gone on on water, from us, from the European Union, from other states."

-Secretary of State Condoleezza Rice, June 2005

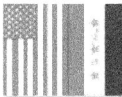

Help Iraq Strengthen Its Economy

STRATEGIC OBJECTIVE: Iraqi government policies and legal framework support a market economy and robust private sector-led growth.

<u>Status</u>: Iraq has enormous economic potential, with an educated, young, and skilled work force and vast natural resources. But Iraq is struggling to reach its economic potential due largely to decades of dictatorship and neglect. Unemployment is high, which fuels popular dissatisfaction and may generate sympathy for the insurgency among some Iraqis. Changing these economic realities will require tough reforms, political will by the Iraqi government, a shift in expectations by the Iraqi people, and the help of the international community. Despite these challenges, Iraq's economy is growing, supporting new businesses every month. Through persistent diplomatic and financial efforts, Iraq is getting control of its once-enormous debt burden. Inflation remains in check, and the international financial institutions have expressed their confidence that Iraq is on the right track.

<u>The United States is helping Iraq achieve this objective through the following lines of action</u>:

- Helping Iraq to improve its fiscal management and transparency

- Encouraging pro-market oriented reform and the achievement of a stable macroeconomic environment

- Supporting the development and implementation of laws and institutions that encourage sustained economic growth

- Encouraging the removal of regulations and termination of practices that obstruct private sector growth in Iraq

- Providing technical assistance to aid the rapid improvement of Iraq's business climate and Iraq's accession to the World Trade Organization

- Assisting the Iraqi government in strengthening its banking and financial system

- Supporting the revitalization of agriculture and other productive sectors to diversify a single-resource-based economy

"... The success of building the new Iraq includes ... the process of political change, which in Iraq is well on the way with the elections and inclusive government, and now a constitutional commission leading to the new constitution and referendum later in the year. But also an economic dimension, for reconstruction and creating opportunity and hope for the Iraqi people..."

- Deputy Secretary of State Robert Zoellick, July 2005

Help Iraq Strengthen the Rule of Law and Promote Civil Rights

STRATEGIC OBJECTIVE: Iraq reforms its legal system and develops institutions capable of addressing threats to public order. Iraq's government operates consistent with internationally recognized standards for civil rights and the rule of law.

Status: The "rule of law" as a concept denotes a government of laws, and not men. It is a concept that was born in Iraq, thousands of years ago, and also eviscerated there, over the past three decades, by Saddam Hussein. Iraq is now trying to reclaim its proud history. It is working to overcome the effects of tyranny by building a legal system that instills confidence in a new government, ensures that every person accused of a crime receives due process – including fair, public, and transparent trials – and a prison system that complies fully with international standards. The steps taken thus far include establishment of an independent judiciary, creation of the Central Criminal Court of Iraq and the Iraq Higher Tribunal, renovation and reconstruction of courthouses throughout Iraq, establishment of a reformed Iraq Correctional Service, and construction of modern civilian prison facilities.

The United States is helping Iraq achieve this objective by pursuing the following lines of action:

- Promoting an independent, unbiased, and ethical court system through technical assistance and training of prosecutors, attorneys, and judges

- Assisting in the enhancement of security for judges trying insurgent and terrorist cases

- Providing support to the Iraqi Special Tribunal as it investigates and prosecutes crimes committed by the former regime

- Advising the Ministry of Justice in the development of a centralized organization for the management and oversight of a fair and efficient national correctional system

- Assisting in the establishment of safe and secure correctional facilities for the care, custody, and treatment of persons incarcerated in the Iraqi correctional system

- Establishing an anti-major crimes task force, with FBI agents and other U.S. officials aiding their Iraqi counterparts during investigations of terrorist attacks and assassinations

- Promoting a climate for national reconciliation through fair, effective, and independent judicial institutions

"One of the most important ways to fight terrorism is to promote democracy, and one of the most important ways to promote democracy is the rule of law."

-Attorney General Alberto Gonzales, July 2005

Increase International Support for Iraq

STRATEGIC OBJECTIVE: The international community, countries in the region, and regional organizations support Iraq's attainment of democracy, prosperity, and security.

Status: Saddam Hussein's tyranny, wars of aggression, massive human rights violations, and defiance of Security Council resolutions made Iraq a pariah state. Iraq's nascent democracy is transforming itself into a fully functioning, engaged, and responsible member of the international community. Iraq has begun to rebuild its relationships with its neighbors and engage the international community. A series of international conferences and the steady development of Iraq's diplomatic relationships have greatly assisted this process. The June 2005 Brussels conference on Iraq, for example, was co-sponsored by the United States and the European Union, and attended by more than 80 countries and international organizations, demonstrating Iraq's revitalized international standing. The enactment in November of U.N. Security Council Resolution 1637, which reaffirmed unanimous support for Iraq's political process and the role of Coalition Forces in Iraq, provides strong international backing to Iraq's transition. So too does Resolution 1618, which unanimously condemned the terrorists operating in Iraq and called upon all nations to support the Iraqi government and stop the flow of terrorists into Iraq.

The United States is helping Iraq achieve this objective by pursuing the following lines of action:

- Encouraging NATO's continued participation in Iraq

- Maximizing international donor reconstruction assistance and the numbers of partners committed to the rebuilding of Iraq, particularly by helping Iraq seek prompt disbursement of previous pledges and forgiveness of debt

- Encouraging further UN involvement in Iraq

- Emphasizing the importance of Syrian cooperation with the Iraqi government, including the interdiction of foreign fighters trying to cross the border

- Fostering lasting relationships between Iraq, regional partners, and neighboring countries to promote greater levels of cooperation and security within Iraq and within the Middle East

"The work that America and our allies have undertaken, and the sacrifices we have made, have been difficult, and necessary, and right. Now is the time to build on these achievements, to make the world safer, and to make the world more free. We must use American diplomacy to help create a balance of power in the world that favors freedom. The time for diplomacy is now."

-Secretary of State Condoleezza Rice, January 2005

Strengthen Public Understanding of Coalition Efforts and Public Isolation of the Insurgents

STRATEGIC OBJECTIVE: Widespread understanding in Iraq, the Arab world, and international arena of Iraq's successes in building democracy, prosperity, and security. Violent extremism is discredited within and outside Iraq. A professional and informative Iraqi news media has taken root.

Status: Successes in Iraq's political and economic development are overshadowed in the international media, including popular pan-Arab outlets, by a relentless focus on terrorist and extremist violence and a misleading spotlight on the disagreements among Iraqi politicians. This has contributed to an inaccurate and unbalanced view of developments in Iraq among many international audiences and within Iraq itself. Since the fall of Saddam, hundreds of new independent media outlets have sprung up in Iraq. Their presence is a testament to the vitality of a free press, but their quality is often uneven and their level of professionalism could be improved. Together with our international partners, we are working to promote civic understanding and enable Iraq's public and private media institutions to flower.

The United States is helping Iraq achieve this objective by pursuing the following lines of action:

- Communicating with the Iraqi public through information programs and civic education campaigns

- Providing technical assistance and training to support a free, independent, and responsible Iraqi media (including television, radio, and print) that delivers high-quality content and responsible reporting throughout Iraq

- With our international partners, working to help the Iraqi Government develop the ability and capacity to communicate with its citizens in a professional, effective, and open manner

- Encouraging Iraqis to participate in the political process, including the referendum on the constitution and national elections in December 2005, through a wide variety of civic education and public communications tools

- Informing Iraqis about the progress of reconstruction, security, and infrastructure on the national, regional, and local level

"America will not impose our own style of government on the unwilling. Our goal instead is to help others find their own voice, to attain their own freedom and to make their own way."

-President George W. Bush, January 2005